Some Vikings decided to move away from their homelands. They sailed west and settled in Iceland and Greenland. Some went as far as North America.

Others went south to England and Europe. They stole treasures and took people as slaves. Some explored eastward and traded furs, honey and weapons for silver, spices and glass.

A brooch

Vikings wore brooches to hold their clothes in place. Women used two oval brooches. Men used one round brooch to fasten their cloaks.

You will need:

Kitchen foil	Dessert spoon	Glue
Golden beads	Safety pin	Cardboard

Follow the steps . . .

1. Crumple up some kitchen foil. Press it firmly into the spoon to give it a rounded shape.

2. Glue on some golden beads.

3. Glue a circle of cardboard on the back. Tape on a safety pin.

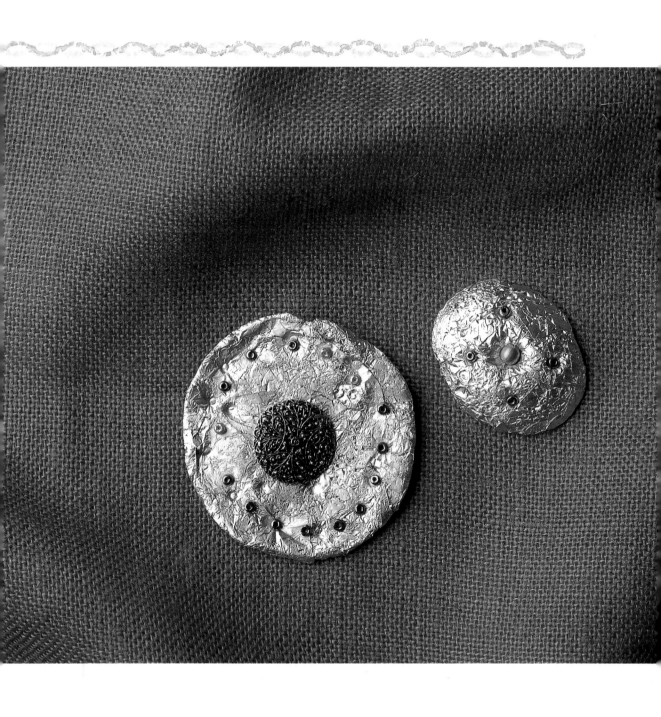

A Viking warrior

The Vikings were fearless warriors. They wore chain mail or padded tunics and carried a sharp sword.

You will need:

Scissors	Card	Glue
Coloured paper	Pencil	Wool
Silver foil	Felt scraps	Paint

Follow the steps . . .

1. Draw a Viking figure on the card. Cut it out. Give it a face.

2. Glue on strands of wool for hair.

3. Cut out a helmet and a silver foil tunic. Glue them on to your Viking.

4. Glue the Viking on to some painted card. Give him a card sword and shield.

Viking homes

Viking families lived and worked in low, dark, smoky longhouses.

The walls were made of woven twigs, covered with thick mud to make them warm and waterproof. This is called wattle and daub.

There was very little furniture. People sat and slept on raised platforms of earth built along the walls. They kept their clothes in wooden chests. Cooking was done over an open fire. A hole in the roof let out the smoke.

A Viking longhouse

You will need:

Shoe box	Scissors	Card
Paints	Paintbrush	Glue

Follow the steps . . .

1. Paint the shoe box brown. Paint a door at one end.

2. Cut a card roof as long as the shoe box and twice as wide. Paint it. Cut a smoke hole.

3. Cut and paint two card triangles with bases slightly wider than the shoe box. Cut the corners off each triangle.

4. Bend over all three edges of each triangle. Glue the base edge to each end of the box.

5. Bend the roof in half. Glue it to the other two edges of the triangles.

Longships

The Vikings built wooden ships which were light, strong and fast. They had a big square sail, and oars for rowing down rivers. A large, heavy oar at the back was used for steering. A fierce animal head, called a figurehead, was carved at the front of the ship.

12

There was room for about thirty oarsmen.
Each man packed his clothes and weapons
into a chest and sat on it. On long journeys
they ate dried fish, hard bread and salted meat.
The Vikings had no maps or instruments.
They used the sun and stars to guide them.

A dragon figurehead

You will need:

Cardboard tube	Newspaper	PVA glue
Sticky tape	Paints	Paintbrush

Follow the steps . . .

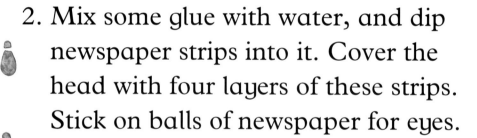

1. Crumple up some newspaper. Shape it into a dragon's head. Tape it together. Push the neck into one end of the cardboard tube.

2. Mix some glue with water, and dip newspaper strips into it. Cover the head with four layers of these strips. Stick on balls of newspaper for eyes.

3. Let the head dry for a few days.

4. Paint the head brown all over. Add eyes and swirling black patterns.

An axe and a shield

You will need:

Corrugated card   Scissors   Cardboard
Cardboard tube   Paint and brush   Glue
Jam jar lid   Sticky tape   Pencil

Follow the steps . . .

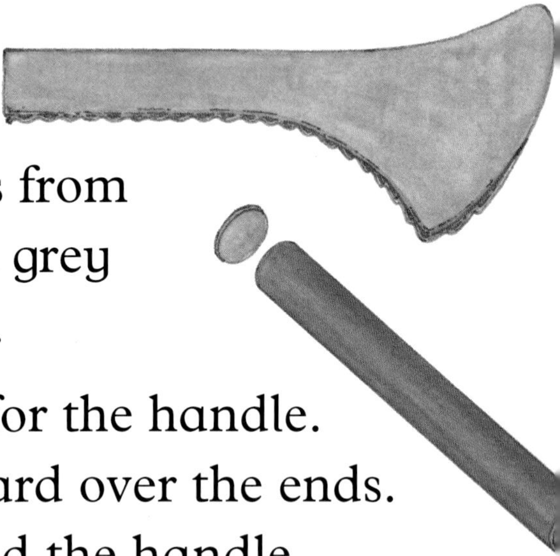

An axe

1. Cut an axe head like this from corrugated card. Paint it grey and add a Viking design.

2. Paint a cardboard tube for the handle. Glue painted circles of card over the ends. Glue the axe head around the handle.

A shield

1. Cut a large circle of corrugated card. Paint it. Glue a painted jam jar lid in the middle.

2. Cut a strip of card for the handle. Bend it and tape it on to the back.

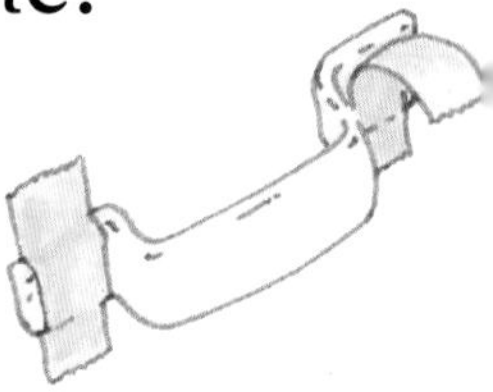

Viking gods

The Vikings worshipped many different gods. They believed that these gods lived in a place called Asgard, which floated above the Earth. They thought that each god was in charge of a particular thing, such as war or weather.

Odin, the god of war, was the ruler of Asgard. He was very fierce and very wise. Wednesday is named after him.

Thor, the god of thunder, was big and strong. He rode across the sky in a chariot. Thursday is named after him.

Viking warriors believed that if they were killed in battle, they would go to a hall in Asgard, called Valhalla. They thought that in Valhalla they would be able to fight all day and feast all night.

Frey was the god of nature. He made sure that the crops grew and the sun shone.

Freyja was Frey's twin sister. She was the goddess of love, beauty and death. Friday is named after her.

Thor's hammer

Viking men wore the symbol of Thor's hammer round their necks to protect themselves against evil spirits.

You will need:

Self-hardening clay   Ballpoint pen   Spoon
Wooden board   Cord or ribbon

Follow the steps . . .

1. Flatten some clay on a board. Cut out the shape of Thor's hammer.

2. Press around the edge of the hammer with the spoon handle to make a border.

3. Use the tip of the ballpoint pen to press a pattern in the hammer.

4. Make a hole in the top of the hammer. Thread the cord or ribbon through it.

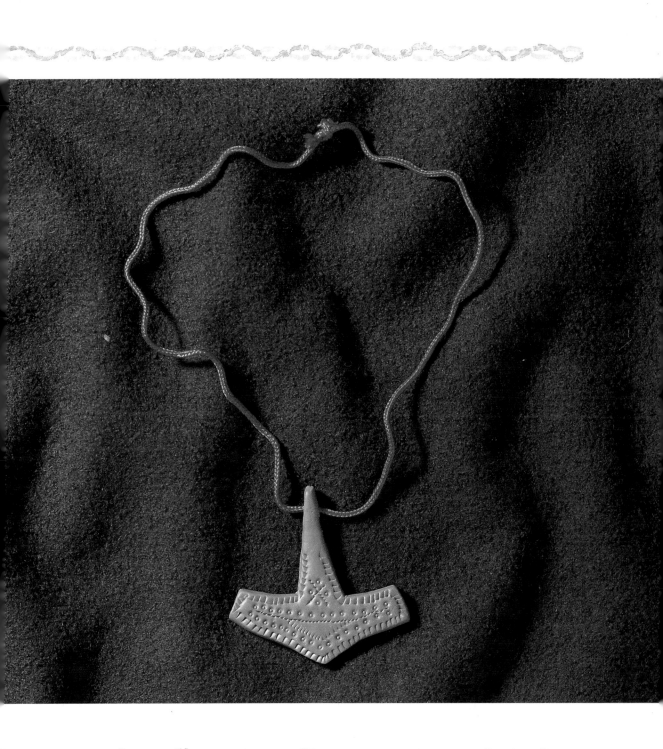

A rune plaque

Viking letters were called runes. This is the alphabet.

ᚨᛒᚲᛞᚨ ᚠᚠᚷ ᚼ ᛁ ᛕᚱᛉ ᚼᛁᚲᚱᚱ᛭ᛏ ᚦ ᚠᛉᛊ

A B C D E F G H I K L M N O P Q R S T U V W X Y Z

The straight lines were easy to carve in stone.
The Vikings carved rune stones in memory of brave
warriors who had been killed in battle.

You will need:

Cardboard   Side plate   Pencil

Paints   Paintbrush   Scissors

Follow the steps . . .

1. Draw round the plate on to the cardboard.
   Cut out the circle you have made.

2. Paint it grey. Write the Viking alphabet
   round the edge. Write your name in the
   middle using runes.

INDEX
Entries in *italics* are activity pages

alphabet 22
Asgard 18, 19
axe and shield 16

battles 19, 22
brooch 4

chain mail 6
clothes 4, 9, 13
cooking 9

Denmark 2
dragon figurehead
12, 14

England 3
Europe 3
evil spirits 20

figureheads 12, 14
food 13
Frey 19

Freyja 19
furniture 9
furs 3

glass 3
gods 18-19
Greenland 3

homeland 3
homes 8-9
honey 3

Iceland 3

longhouse 10
longships 12-13

North America 3
Norway 2

oars 12
Odin 18

rune plaque 22
rune stones 22
runes 22

sail 12
silver 3
slaves 3
spices 3
Sweden 2
swords 6

Thor 18, 20
Thor's hammer 20
trading 3
tunics 6

Valhalla 19
Viking warrior 6

wattle and daub 8
weapons 3, 6, 13, 16

© 1995 Franklin Watts
This edition 2001

Franklin Watts
96 Leonard Street
London EC2A 4XD

Franklin Watts Australia
56 O'Riordan Street
Alexandria, Sydney
NSW 2015

ISBN 0 7496 4172 X

Dewey Decimal Classification
Number 948

A CIP catalogue record for this
book is available from the British
Library.

10 9 8 7 6 5 4 3 2 1

Editor: Annabel Martin
Consultant: Richard Tames
Design: Mike Davis
Artwork: Cilla Eurich
          Ruth Levy
Photographs: Peter Millard

Printed in Malaysia

THE Vikings

Ruth Thomson

Contents

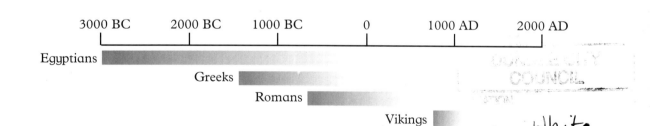

3000 BC   2000 BC   1000 BC   0   1000 AD   2000 AD

Egyptians

Greeks

Romans

Vikings

W
FRANKLIN WATTS
LONDON•SYDNEY

Who were the Vikings?

The Vikings lived over one thousand years ago. They settled around the coasts of the countries we now call Norway, Sweden and Denmark.

There was not much good land for farming. Norway was very mountainous. Sweden was covered in thick forest, and much of Denmark was too sandy.

Greenland

Iceland

Newfoundland